SUPER CUTE!

# Baby Rhinos

by Megan Borgert-Spaniol

Blastoff! Readers 1

BELLWETHER MEDIA • MINNEAPOLIS, MN

Note to Librarians, Teachers, and Parents:

**Blastoff! Readers** are carefully developed by literacy experts and combine standards-based content with developmentally appropriate text.

**Level 1** provides the most support through repetition of high-frequency words, light text, predictable sentence patterns, and strong visual support.

**Level 2** offers early readers a bit more challenge through varied simple sentences, increased text load, and less repetition of high-frequency words.

**Level 3** advances early-fluent readers toward fluency through increased text and concept load, less reliance on visuals, longer sentences, and more literary language.

**Level 4** builds reading stamina by providing more text per page, increased use of punctuation, greater variation in sentence patterns, and increasingly challenging vocabulary.

**Level 5** encourages children to move from "learning to read" to "reading to learn" by providing even more text, varied writing styles, and less familiar topics.

Whichever book is right for your reader, Blastoff! Readers are the perfect books to build confidence and encourage a love of reading that will last a lifetime!

This edition first published in 2017 by Bellwether Media, Inc.



Library of Congress Cataloging-in-Publication Data

Names: Borgert-Spaniol, Megan, 1989- , author.
Title: Baby Rhinos / by Megan Borgert-Spaniol.
Description: Minneapolis, MN : Bellwether Media, Inc., 2017. | Series: Blastoff! Readers. Super Cute! | Includes bibliographical references and index. | Audience: Ages 5 to 8. | Audience: Grades K to 3.
Identifiers: LCCN 2016032028 (print) | LCCN 2016038136 (ebook) | ISBN 9781626175464 (hardcover : alk. paper) | ISBN 9781681032757 (ebook)
Subjects: LCSH: Rhinoceroses–Infancy–Juvenile literature.
Classification: LCC QL737.U63 B667 2017 (print) | LCC QL737.U63 (ebook) | DDC 599.66/81392–dc23
LC record available at https://lccn.loc.gov/2016032028



Editor: Betsy Rathburn Designer: Brittany McIntosh

Printed in the United States of America, North Mankato, MN.

# Table of Contents

# Rhino Calf!

A baby rhino is called a calf. A **newborn** calf can weigh more than 100 pounds (45 kilograms)!

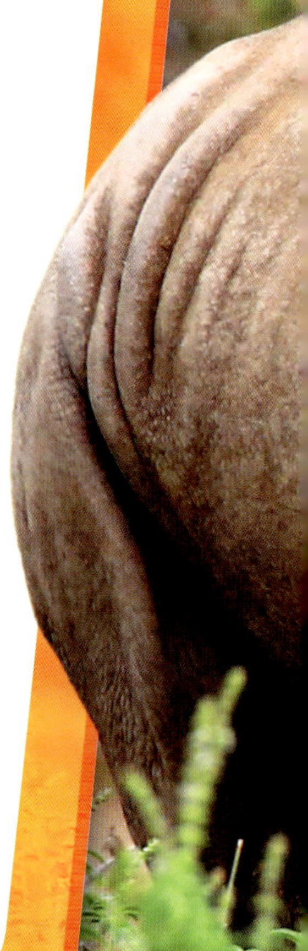

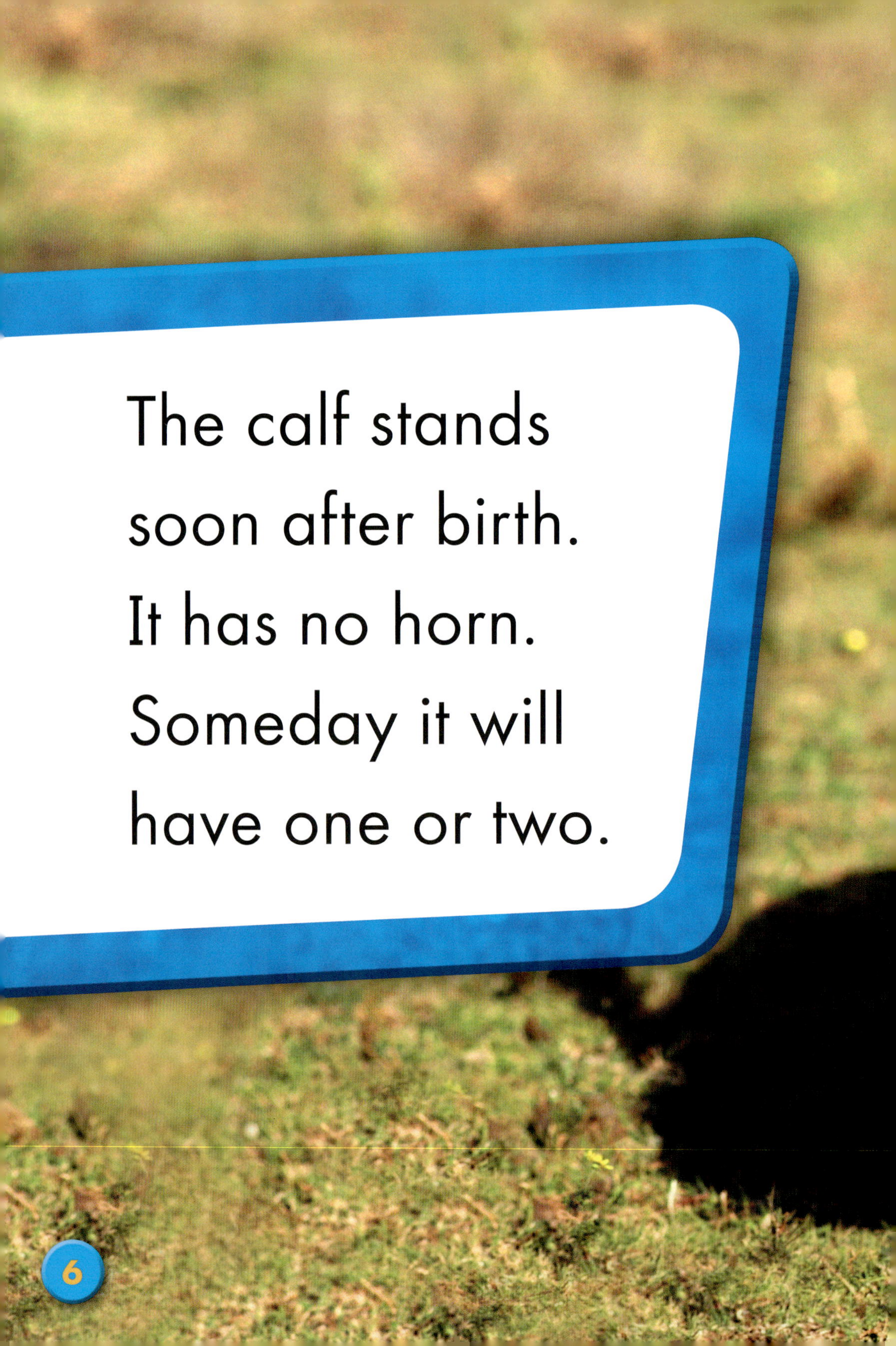

The calf stands soon after birth. It has no horn. Someday it will have one or two.

# Life With Mom

Mom **nuzzles** her baby to show love.

Mom and her calf rest in shade during the day.

They also **wallow** in mud. This protects their skin from sun and bugs.

Mom keeps her calf safe. She scares away **predators**.

The calf **nurses** when hungry. It also chews on plants.

## Joining the Crash

Sometimes mom and calf join a **crash**. They eat and rest in a group.

The calf plays and **spars** with other rhinos. **Charge**!

# Glossary

**charge**—to run forward to attack

**crash**—a group of rhinos

**newborn**—just recently born

**nurses**—drinks mom's milk

**nuzzles**—softly rubs up against with the nose or forehead

**predators**—animals that hunt other animals for food

**spars**—playfully fights; rhinos spar with their horns.

**wallow**—to lie or roll around in mud or water

# To Learn More

## AT THE LIBRARY

Doudna, Kelly. *It's a Baby Rhinoceros!* Edina, Minn.: ABDO Publishing Company, 2009.

Mattern, Joanne. *Rhinoceroses.* Mankato, Minn.: Pebble Books, 2010.

Schuetz, Kari. *Rhinoceroses.* Minneapolis, Minn.: Bellwether Media, 2012.

## ON THE WEB

Learning more about rhinos is as easy as 1, 2, 3.

1. Go to www.factsurfer.com.
2. Enter "rhinos" into the search box.
3. Click the "Surf" button and you will see a list of related web sites.

With factsurfer.com, finding more information is just a click away.

# Index




The images in this book are reproduced through the courtesy of: Eric Isselee, front cover; Reinhold Leitner, pp. 4-5; Jonathan Pledger, pp. 6-7; Gerard Lacz/ Age Fotostock, pp. 8-9; Jurgen & Christine Sohns/ FLPA/ Glow Images, pp. 10-11; FLPA/ SuperStock, pp. 12-13; NHPA/ SuperStock, pp. 14-15; Nataiki, pp. 16-17; wildestanimal, pp. 18-19; Alamy, pp. 20-21.